Fun
to
LEARn

Just the Job

Written by Kate Tym • Illustrated by Deborah Allwright

The story and all the pictures
in this book are original
and have been specially
commissioned for Tesco.

Published by
Tesco Stores Limited
Created by Brilliant Books Ltd
84-86 Regent Street
London W1B 5RR
www.brilliantbooks.co.uk

First published 2001

Text and illustrations © 2001
Brilliant Books Ltd
Printed by Printer Trento S.r.l., Italy
Reproduction by Graphic Ideas Studios

ISBN 1-84221-149-8

1 3 5 7 9 10 8 6 4 2

Geronimo, Spike, Toby,
Morris and Zak were friends...
who all did different jobs.

Zak worked as a postman delivering mail.

Morris was an optician.

But he often wondered if it was the right job for him.

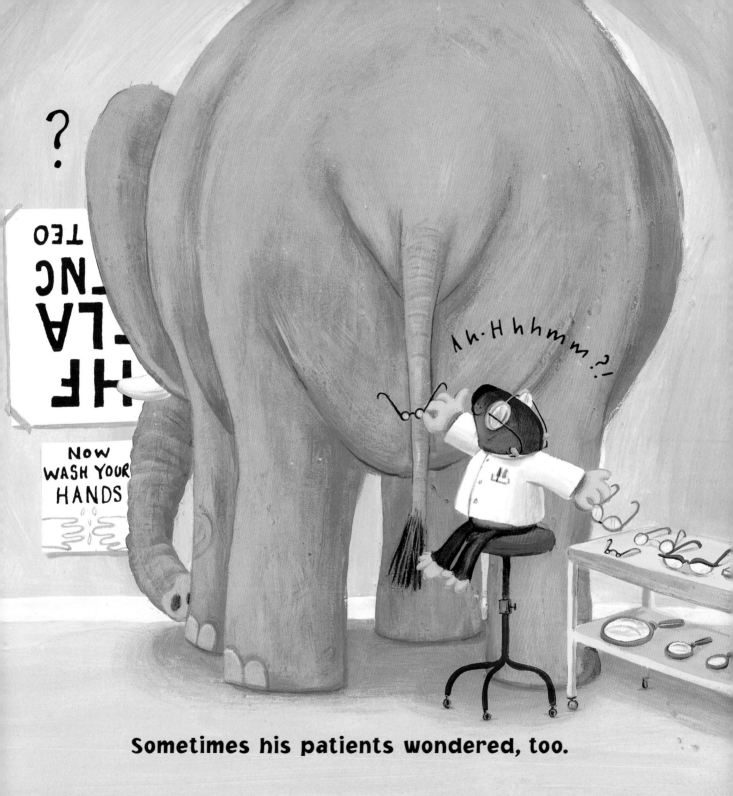

Sometimes his patients wondered, too.

Geronimo worked in the china section of a really posh department store...

£££

wibble

Toby delivered pizzas for a living...

...very...very...slowly.

And Spike was a quality checker in a balloon factory.

But he wasn't very popular
with his fellow workers.

Then one day...all five friends got the sack.

You're

Fired!

They met down at the job centre.